HOW TO HAVE THE FINAL SAY

The tools you need to win any argument

Written by Benjamin Fléron

Translated by Carly Probert

Coaching **50MINUTES**.com

50MINUTES.com

PROPEL
YOUR BUSINESS FORWARD!

NETWORKING

Effective CV Writing

Resolving Office Conflict

Boost Your Concentration

Find Your Work-Life Balance

www.50minutes.com

HOW TO ALWAYS HAVE THE FINAL SAY

- **Problem:** How can I emerge victorious from a verbal confrontation using appropriate dialogue and the correct tone?
- **Uses:** Enable yourself to defend your opinions, demonstrate your worth and maintain your professional credibility.
- **Professional context:** Human resources, personal development, professional relationships.
- **FAQs:**
  - Are we born quick-witted?
  - Does everyone have the ability to give quick comebacks?
  - What is the difference between good and bad debating?
  - What attitude should be adopted to ensure maximum chances for success?
  - What advantages can I obtain from developing my debating skills?
  - How can I improve my debating abilities?
  - A colleague often teases me about my appearance, how can I respond?
  - How can I respond to my boss without the risk of getting on the wrong side of them?

Whether after a heated debate among colleagues, after a scathing remark from your employer or on leaving a job interview, perhaps you have already asked yourself the following question: "Why on earth didn't I say that at the time?". But whether it was an appropriate response to quiet someone, a rhetorical dodge to avoid an embarrassing question or a touch of humour to defuse a tense situation, the right reply always come to us once the battle is over, and often lost. Frustrated at not being able to defend yourself as well as you would have liked, humiliated at being bettered in public without knowing how to react, you are then re-duced to beating yourself up about your lack of comebacks. "If only it could be taught!" you say. But who ever said it couldn't be?

Contrary to what some perhaps some still imagine, debating skills are not innate. It is not a blessing bestowed upon a select few, inherited at birth, and there is no debating gene that may or may not appear in our DNA. So why can some people always manage to come out with great responses without even looking like they are trying, while others inevitably end up tripping up whenever they try to be witty? Often, they simply have not lived the same life course. Therefore, the reasons for which they react differently to similar situations can be very varied: the environment in which they grew up and developed, their experiences, the encounters they have had or even, potentially, training to develop and gradually improve their debating skills.

Learning this art is not restricted to an elite few or to certain types of individuals. Everyone can indeed acquire debating abilities if they wish to do so, for example by learning to control their emotions, through learning improvisation, expanding their vocabulary and collection of go-to replies, or drawing inspiration from the leading experts on the subject. So whether you are introverted or extroverted, highly educated or not, wherever you are from, you too can become a specialist in debate, a professional at dry humour and an expert on counterattacks, as long as you make the necessary efforts. No more excuses – get stuck in!

DEBATING: THE BASICS

WHAT ARE ITS USES IN THE WORLD OF WORK?

Although it also proves useful in many situations of everyday life, debating can be particularly valuable and beneficial in the workplace. Consider an employee buried under a pile of paperwork, fearing he may lose his job if he offends his boss and not daring to say anything when the latter gives him yet another task; or a worker, however competent he may be, who cannot bring himself to say no when backed into a corner by his recruiter. Also imagine a boss who is losing client after client because she never manages to justify why the various tasks are falling behind. Finally, imagine how a colleague must feel when they are responsible for an important presentation, and stutter sadly in response to a question asked by their supervisor. Many people would never find themselves in such awful situations if only they had developed their debating skills.

Improving your rhetorical talents and improvisation abilities has many advantages on a professional level, and can also have an extremely beneficial impact on your career and your wellbeing at work. Thus, learning to respond to provocations and difficult questions will help you to be more comfortable when it comes to:

- Delivering a presentation to a large audience, whether it is made up of clients, colleagues or managers. You will never have to worry about comments or questions be-

cause you will always have the correct responses to hand.
- Justifying a delay or error. Whether the fault is entirely your own or not, you will always find the proper way to spin the situation to get out of this kind of predicament.
- Imposing your presence and your ideas on your colleagues. You will no longer be an anonymous and invisible employee, squashed by stronger personalities, but a full member of the team and an important part of its daily operations.
- Establishing your authority and earning the respect of your employees without having to be tyrannical. A boss or supervisor who cannot win without inspiring fear among his subordinates will not be respected and will quickly be abandoned by them in times of hardship.
- Succeeding in interviews and stress resistance tests which are likely to be given by recruiters. By maintaining your composure in all circumstances, recruiters will be more easily convinced that you are the most qualified person for the job.
- Winning contracts from potential customers. If you have the answers to all of their questions and manage to reassure them about their concerns, why wouldn't they choose you to protect their interests?

These are just a few of the potential professional benefits that can be derived from sharp debating abilities. For those who acquaint themselves with this delicate and precious art, the benefits can also be felt in everyday life, through increased self-confidence, newfound serenity, easier sociability, etc. Therefore, there is no reason for anyone not to learn this skill.

Before trying to master the expertise of a good response, it is important to ask one fundamental question, as its answer is not as obvious as it sounds: is a good response always necessarily aggressive and does it aim to silence the opponent? Would a softer response not ease an opponent who is slightly too irritable and stifle a potential conflict – would this type of response not be just as effective? Finally, what about a humorous twist that would allow you to skilfully dodge an embarrassing question? Which of these attitudes should we opt for?

In truth, there is no one type of response that is better than another or that can be used in any circumstances. There is no magic formula that will always be effective. This might be stating the obvious, but ultimately, good debating skills are the only solution. So what factors are important for helping you choose the most appropriate response?

Factors to consider	Situation
The status and personality of your opponent. You do not respond in the same way to a colleague whom you know well, and who has the same 'rank' as you, as you do to your new employer, whom you are just getting to know and to whom you have to answer. You must take into account the personality of the person you are facing: it is not because you are under the direct orders of the manager that he will not be receptive to frank and direct observation. Following this logic, not everyone reacts in the same way to the same type of humour. Two colleagues may react differently to light teasing; black humour may work well with one person, while schoolboy humour will fall completely flat with that same person. Thus, it is important to know first who you are talking to if you want to adapt your response.	*Robert, with whom you have worked for almost 10 years and who you consider to be a friend, teases you about the few kilos you put on over the holidays. Robert is not very tall and is used to self-mockery, so you do not hesitate to respond that you took the extra few centimetres he lacks in height and put them on your waist! Robert laughs: he had it coming. Hours later, you make the same comment to Roger, who is the same height as Robert, but has a complex about his height. Obviously you expect the same reaction, but Roger reacts much worse than Robert. Finally, Eric, the new department head, asks you with a smile if you overdid the turkey at Christmas. Eric seems rather friendly and you know he is joking, but he remains your superior and you don't know him well enough to 'return the serve', so you just smile and say that a small diet certainly wouldn't do you any harm.*

Factors to consider	Situation
The tone used by your opponent. It is not enough to simply listen to what they say, you also need to pay particular attention to their tone. Are they angry? At you personally or at the situation you cannot change? Are they gently teasing you or are they trying to hurt you? Are they attacking you or giving measured responses to what you say? By answering these questions, you will be able to choose the right tone with which to respond. This will stop you from overreacting, which could be perceived as paranoia or a lack of self-confidence, and may lead to you stumbling on your words, weakening your credibility.	*Electricians, Mark and Fred, install electrical systems in old houses. After having provided the expected service, they give the bill to their respective clients, who both have the same reaction: "It's crazy how the cost of living is rising. 10 years ago, this bill would have been half as cheap!" Mark nods and smiles: "That's true...luckily I work twice as well!" The customer also smiles and keeps Mark's number. Fred, meanwhile, feels insulted by this remark: "Are you calling me a thief?", "No, you misunderstood me!" replies the customer, who quickly pays to prove his good faith. Fred leaves annoyed while the customer, taken aback by the excessive reaction of Fred, will not call him to work again.*

Factors to consider	Situation
The context in which the interaction takes place. Is it an informal discussion by the coffee machine or an important meeting with employees? Are clients present or is it an internal meeting? Has the other party's day been excessively difficult, to the point where you can ignore their bad mood as you know they are not thinking through what they are saying? Some situations may require humour while in others it may be unsuitable, just as there are times when you get straight to the point, and others where it is better to get your message across more subtly.	*The day is coming to an end while Paul is putting the finishing touches to a file for the next day. John, his superior, suddenly appears in his office to reproach him for his slowness, saying that he should have finished this file yesterday (even though he wasn't told this until today). However, John does not usually shout at his staff like this, even less so without good reason. Paul prepares to retaliate in the same tone when he recalls that this afternoon John was responsible for settling a far more important issue for his boss. If the rumours he heard are anything to go by, the meeting did not go well. Paul understands the mood of John better and opts for a strategy: he calmly explains that he understands his anger, but it should not be directed at him, he only received the file today and he did his best to finish it as quickly as possible. John admits his error and regains composure.*

Factors to consider	Situation
Your personality. By developing your debating skills, you are adding new strings to your bow, and will perhaps change your image in the eyes of others who notice your evolution. This is inevitable and is not necessarily a bad thing. However, avoid going too far and acting like someone you are not. Don't force yourself to use a certain type of humour if you do not like it and have never laughed at this kind of joke before. Start with small, humorous remarks that match your personality more. Similarly, do not suddenly act like a tough guy if you have always had a soft character. Assert yourself more and more, don't let others walk all over you, without however being threatening towards your opponent. It is up to you to work out what suits you best, what you are comfortable with and how you feel. For a response to be effective it must be delivered confidently and naturally. You will not convince anyone if it looks like you are forcing yourself.	*Peter never says no, and his colleagues have become accustomed to offloading many of their obligations onto him without even realising it. So when the end of the day comes, Peter is exhausted and has to settle the problems of others as well as his own. Peter says that he is probably too nice and he should change his ways. He does not know what to do but understands that his extreme kindness is the source of his problems. Peter therefore sees the opposite behaviour as the solution to all his problems. He then becomes convinced that he must play the bad guy, but his first attempts all fail. He cannot act in a way that completely contradicts his personality and his character, and is not very convincing. Peter feels ridiculous and quickly returns to his old ways.*

SOME FAMOUS DEBATERS

- Lady Astor (British politician, 1879-1964) disagreed with Winston Churchill (1874-1965), exclaiming: "Winston, if I were your wife, I would put poison in your tea!" Churchill's response: "If I were your

husband, I'd drink it!"
- Albert Einstein (1879-1955) and Charlie Chaplin (1889-1997): "What I admire most about your art, is its universality. You do not say a word and yet the world understands you." "It's true," replied Chaplin, "But your fame is even greater. The world admires you, when nobody understands you!"
- Hardy, comedian, addressing his companion, Laurel: "But you've completely emptied the glass. We were supposed to share half and half." Laurel replies: "I couldn't help it, my half was at the bottom."

THE RIGHT ATTITUDE

A response that works in all circumstances does not exist, however it is imperative to know some essential points to make your responses effective. By keeping these in mind, you will already have made a huge step towards mastering this practice.

Trust yourself

As we have just seen, a response has much more of a chance of achieving its goal if said with confidence and conviction. Your attitude is essential, perhaps even more so than the sentence itself. Also, be sure of yourself and don't be afraid of losing your head. Keep your chin up, shake yourself off and dive in! In the words of Michael Audiard, a great man of French cinema, "an intellectual sitting down always makes less progress than a stupid person who is walking", meaning a bad response delivered with conviction will always have more weight than a good response that is merely mumbled with apprehension!

GOOD TO KNOW

Be aware of your strengths and weaknesses. Accepting them allows you to make use of them, including through self-mockery, to rely on your strengths and to make up for your flaws.

Stay relaxed

A good response must not give the impression that your life depends on it. Don't take yourself too seriously! Although we often talk about a 'response', a 'confrontation' or a 'verbal attack', learn to consider this exchange like a game, not as an armed conflict. Relax, have fun and, above all, smile! What could be more disarming? This is the best proof that any dirty tricks aimed at you will not affect you, since you know what you are worth and you give more credit to your own judgement than that of a third party. As a bonus, you will be much more natural and relaxed, and will therefore find it easier to find the right words to express yourself.

Stay spontaneous and take a step back

"Here lies the difficulty!" you say. Indeed, this is where problems arise most often. The perfectly appropriate response often comes to mind eventually...but usually a bit too late. The solution is simple: stop focusing on finding the perfect answer! Listen carefully to the other person, identify the intent behind their words and respond naturally.

By focusing on the other person, their attitude, their tone and their words, you will no longer be focused on yourself and will distance yourself a little from the situation. You will therefore be more able to respond spontaneously without being overcome by your emotions. It is no accident that you cannot think of the perfect answer in the heat of the moment, but that it springs to mind once the tension has subsided. This is because you have had time to step back and your emotions have subsided, giving way to reason. Although this is not obvious, good responses require you to detach yourself from the conversation.

Pay attention to your body language

Do not underestimate the importance of body language in the success of your exchange. Posture and gestures say more about you and your state of mind that you think, so pay particular attention to them unless you want to see your best responses fall flat. However, weighing up your every move is obviously not possible or recommended (you do not want to look like a robot!), and the experts themselves sometimes struggle to agree on the significance of a particular gesture. Fortunately, there is nonetheless a series of postures and physical instinctive reflexes that do not lie and of which you should be wary. For example, crossing your arms during a verbal attack will reveal your discomfort with your partner as strongly as if you started to stutter.

Instead, try to adopt a more open posture with straight

shoulders, arms beside your body and your feet apart. You will look much more confident. If you do not succeed, make a habit of placing your thumbs in your belt loops to keep yourself from crossing your arms and maintain a permanently open posture. Similarly, pay attention to the things you may do without even realising it, but which will betray you every time:

- Avoiding the eyes of your partner when you are lying to them;
- Touching your nose whenever you are uncomfortable;
- Tapping your foot on the ground when you are nervous or stressed;
- Biting your lip or yours nails when you are anxious.

Rest assured, there is no need to become a specialist in order to avoid committing these harmful errors. Simply identify your own habits and mannerisms and dedicate yourself to making them disappear one after the other.

TOP TIPS

- **Tune in!** This is the best advice you can apply. Indeed, in order to know what and how to respond to your opponent, you must first understand their message and listen carefully. As we have already mentioned, you must not only pay attention to their words, but also to the tone they use, their gestures, their expressions, etc. What message are they trying to convey? What is the intent behind it? What are the flaws in their speech that could be exploited to your advantage? Finally, be on the lookout for good words, flashes of humour, ingenious phrases, etc., either in real life or on television. You hear them every day, so why not use them yourself? This is the easiest way to expand your stock of responses.
- **Practice!** There is no miracle: replies do not fall from heaven, and you will not become an expert in scathing responses and dodges within five minutes. Like everything that is learned, it requires time, training and implementation. Note the responses that you like and repeat them until they sound natural. Repeat them in front of your mirror if necessary (no one will see you!) and test them in real conditions. Analyse their impact, what worked and what did not. Similarly, instead of avoiding debates for fear of looking foolish, get used to participating. This is the only way you will start to progress. Does this scare you? Nothing is stopping you from doing things slowly, starting by taking part in discussions with less important subjects and which are not so emotionally charged. TV shows, sports event or current trends are perfect training

ground to begin to express your opinions and test your abilities. Soon, you will know what sentences earn you points, as well as those that are less effective, or when you should speak up and when to be more cool and detached.

- **Be inspired!** Certain categories of people are renowned for always knowing what to say, so why not take inspiration from them? For example, acting professionals benefit from practicing improvisation, but also theatrical expression, allowing them to physically impose themselves and occupy space in a way that few people are able to. In addition, they usually have a significant literary culture on which they can rely. Politicians are also known to bounce back and respond quickly to the different verbal spears thrown at them. Moreover, they are masters in the art of dodging issues that may put them in awkward positions. So get clued up on political debates and interviews and take hints from them! Finally, do not forget that we are in the era of the famous 'snipers' of television. Whether they are recognised critics or simply comedians, they are known for their lightning-quick responses and not letting people push them around.

EXTRA INFORMATION

By watching their actions, you can freely explore the behaviour of their designated 'victims'. Can they cope? Are they keeping pace? If yes, how? If not, what attitudes are putting them at a disadvantage?

- **Don't be overwhelmed by your emotions!** This is probably one of the hardest pieces of advice to follow, but also one of the most important. Indeed, what could be more human than reacting emotionally to what we perceive as an assault or a personal attack? If the subject is close to your heart, it's even harder to detach. However, it is imperative that you learn to keep your cool and control your nerves, at the risk of losing your composure. Remember: you are not putting your life on the line, so do not panic unnecessarily! This is the only way you will manage to use all your intellectual resources in record time.

- **Work on your physical approach!** This cannot be said enough: the way in which you deliver your response is at least as important as the response itself. Keep in mind that the form is paramount and a response will not have the same impact if you mumble it with your hand over your mouth, your chin on your chest and shifting eyes, as a response that is delivered with your head high, shoulders back, a smile on your face and eye contact. Body language says more about you than you might think, and the outcome of a debate often depends on it. Feel free to take acting classes, as there is no better way to find out more about your body language and learn to make it a valuable ally.

- **Believe you can win!** You will never emerge victorious from a verbal confrontation if you are convinced that you will lose before the battle has even begun. You have probably heard of the sporting habit of imagining lifting the trophy before playing the game. This is what we call positive thinking: by imagining your success, repeating it again and again like a mantra, you will create a winning mind-set and thereby create the necessary conditions to get there. Building upon this method, you can build a positive mental picture to which you respond with confidence and coolness in the face of a tough opponent. Thus, by visualising the scene in your mind, you will be much more comfortable and sure of yourself when things really happen.

- **Don't take yourself too seriously!** Use humour and self-mockery, learn to laugh at yourself. You will be all the stronger when it comes to facing criticism and mockery, because they will not affect you. What is more effective than destabilising your opponent by using his own ammunition against yourself, taking great care to defuse it with a smile? Are you smaller than one of your colleagues and he enjoys pointing it out? Tell him that you take on work inversely proportionate to your size. Does he make fun of you for being overweight? Reply with a smile that you can never resist your partner's cooking! Don't hesitate to play on stereotypes. Think of those comedians that voluntarily play on their origin, gender or religion and the prejudice resulting thereof. Jamel Debbouze (comedian from a Parisian suburb and of Moroccan origin, born in 1975) has built his comedy career from clichés about city youths and immigration, while US director Woody Allen (born in 1935) is the first to laugh at the supposed stinginess of Jews, when he is one himself! How can we make fun of them when they are doing it so well themselves?

FAQS

ARE WE BORN QUICK-WITTED?

No one is born with debating skills! They are not innate, inherited or bestowed through the intervention of the Holy Spirit; they are an asset that we acquire and refine through hard work, research, experimentation, practice, failures and successes. Some people have certainly grown up in more favourable environments for the development of this ability: a family of intellectuals, literary studies, a special attraction to humour, etc. This does not mean that they are the only ones able to develop this weapon.

DOES EVERYONE HAVE THE ABILITY TO GIVE QUICK COMEBACKS?

Yes, absolutely anyone can learn to develop their debating skills. Whatever their origin, personality or level of education, a person can always move forward if they make the necessary efforts and show willingness. There is no excuse for not at least trying to improve!

WHAT IS THE DIFFERENCE BETWEEN GOOD AND BAD DEBATING?

The answer to this is simply that one serves its purpose and the other does not. There is no response that is fundamentally good or bad, it is its success that determines this, and this can depend on many factors: the function and the personality of the speaker, their mood, the context in which the interaction takes place, etc. Therefore, the same response may sometimes be good, and other times bad.

WHAT ATTITUDE SHOULD BE ADOPTED TO ENSURE MAXIMUM CHANCES FOR SUCCESS?

The following behaviours facilitate the success of a debate.

- **Self-confidence:** a bad response stated with conviction, while holding eye contact, will always be more likely to achieve its aim than a good response that is mumbled with lowered eyes. In a verbal confrontation, style is always as important as what you say.
- **Humour:** The practice of self-mockery allows you to take a step back from the situation and from yourself and, therefore, to remove the drama involved. This also deprives the opponent of things that they can latch on to. Finally, giving the confrontation moderate importance, you constrain your partner, who would otherwise behave like an excessive and rude person.
- **Letting go:** By not trying to control everything to get the perfect response, you will be more spontaneous in your answers; they will become more natural and therefore stronger. The 'best' is the enemy of 'good', so do not wear yourself out trying to search for the perfect answer and end up not answering anything at all. Just listen to what the other person has to say, without worrying too much about how you are going to argue against it, and proceed with confidence.

WHAT ADVANTAGES CAN I GET FROM DEVELOPING MY DEBATING SKILLS?

The potential benefits are numerous:

- fewer difficulties in justifying a delay or error with your manager;
- more confidence with your clients and therefore more earnings and/or agreements secured;
- more natural authority among your employees;
- more self-confidence when expressing your ideas or exposing the results of your work, thus projecting a better image of yourself within your company;
- more drive and confidence in job interviews, and therefore popularity with recruiters;
- more fluency and ease when speaking in public;
- etc.

HOW CAN I IMPROVE MY DEBATING ABILITIES?

There are many ways to make progress in this area.

- **Watch and listen to your partner:** their words, the message, their mood, body language, etc., to detect possible flaws in their speech, but not focus too much on your own emotions and feelings.
- **Practice again and again:** note words and phrases that you hear and like and practice them in front of a mirror, until they appear to be your "own". In addition, participate in as many debates and discussions as possible, and

improve your vocabulary.

- **Take inspiration from specialists in the field:** stage professionals, politicians, media men, great writers, film dialogue writers, etc.
- **Pay attention to your physical attitude and work on it if necessary:** posture, gestures, tone of voice, facial expressions, etc., all of which can convey positive or negative information about you and influence the scope of your speech.
- **Be confident and sure of your success:** visualise the scene and imagine you are the winner, thus increasing your chances of success.
- **Develop your sense of humour and self-mockery:** laugh at your complexes, your appearance physical traits or stereotypes related to your origin, gender or religion.

A COLLEAGUE OFTEN TEASES ME ABOUT MY APPEARANCE, HOW CAN I RESPOND?

The first thing to do is to not care too much about his remarks, which will only encourage him further. In addition, perhaps he is simply trying to destabilise you and, having no complaints about the quality of your work, is trying another approach. Reacting negatively and answering with aggression means you are entering the game and showing him that what he said has hurt you. Instead, do the opposite: laugh and counter-attack him with a joke. You have no reason to feel ashamed about who you are, so why act as if this is the case?

Learn to play on stereotypes and use them in your favour

when possible. Is a new colleague trying to get noticed by mocking your larger-than-average waistline? Tell him that it's because you ate those that came before him and that his turn will come soon enough. Is he teasing you about your alleged big ears? Tell him that your only regret is that you are forced to listen to all his nonsense. The possibilities are endless, but the principle remains the same: do not be ashamed of who you are, do not try to hide your flaws, but accept them with good humour and use them to tease others in turn!

HOW CAN I RESPOND TO MY BOSS WITHOUT THE RISK OF ALIENATING MYSELF?

Although asserting yourself to a colleague is far from easy, things get even more complicated when it comes to a supervisor who has the power to make your work life miserable, or even fire you. Once again, there is no right or wrong way to react to the situation. However, some procedures are preferable to others. Don't overreact, get carried away by anger or respond aggressively. Instead of adding fuel to the fire and starting a situation you cannot get out of, remain calm and soothe tensions.

As you may have guessed, the use of humour is highly recommended here. Please note, the idea is not to ridicule what the other person is saying (this would just make them angry), but to laugh them off with self-mockery.

OVER TO YOU!

As we have seen, there is unfortunately no exhaustive list of 'magic' responses that you can simply learn by heart and recite at the appropriate time. The correct response on one day will perhaps not be effective the next day, the response that keeps a colleague at bay will not affect your boss and the joke that makes everyone laugh when your friend tells is will perhaps prove disastrous for you.

To find your own style, you have to consider your experiences and realise for yourself what suits you best, what works and what doesn't, and under which circumstances.

Are you a defeatist?	This attitude will not help you, even alongside autosuggestion and visualisation. The next time you are tasked with delivering a presentation to important clients or you must chair a meeting, use the days before it to put this advice in practice. Use free time during the day to play out the scene in your head and turn it to your advantage. Imagine yourself winning and being sure of yourself, ready to respond quickly to any questions that come your way. Repeat to yourself, like a mantra, that you will succeed. Instead of focusing on your failures, make a list of your best successes. By reading these every day, you will believe in yourself and your skills and will therefore create the conditions necessary to succeed.
Do you have a stock of responses that you find hilarious, but fail to make anyone else laugh?	The problem lies in the way you are telling them, work on this to improve. Get inspired by the best comedians with dry humour: watch their shows and TV appearances. Pay particular attention to their intonations, their gestures, their use of pauses, etc. Now practise it yourself. Practise in front of a mirror, or even better, record yourself to listen back to your voice. This exercise gives you distance to assess your performance, so you won't get a false idea of how others hear you.

On the other hand, do you have a strong voice and appearance but your words fail to defend you effectively?	Find inspiration to expand your repertoire. Set a goal, such as reading a set number of books a month or taking more of an interest in different types of debates shown on TV channels.
Finally, there is a fun game you can indulge in if you want to improve your debating skills, whatever your starting level.	Open a dictionary at random and take the first word you see. Read the definition, get a pencil and a sheet of paper and give yourself 10 minutes to write everything the word makes you think of. Once the allotted time has passed, organise your notes in the way that makes the most sense, even if it ultimately is of little interest. Then, restart the stopwatch and try to defend this speech orally until you have nothing left to say. Gradually, you will become more and more comfortable, you will be able to quickly structure your ideas and you will be capable of discussing many different topics.

You are the best person to recognise your flaws and failures, so you just need to identify them and apply the corresponding tips mentioned throughout this book. The only way is up!

We want to hear from you!
Leave a comment on your online library
and share your favourite books on social media!

FURTHER READING

BIBLIOGRAPHY

- Cavelier, Y. (2012) Comment avoir toujours des idées sur n'importe quel sujet et ne plus jamais louper d'opportunités. *Copywriting-Pratique.com.* [Online]. [Accessed 8 August 2015]. Available from: <http://www.copywriting-pratique.com/comment-avoir-toujoursdes-idees-sur-n-importe-quel-sujet-et-ne-plus-jamais-louper-dopportunites/>
- Chaudeau, C. (2013) Comment avoir de la répartie en entretien d'embauche ? *Keljob.com.* [Online]. [Accessed 8 August 2015]. Available from: <http://www.keljob.com/editorial/chercher-un-emploi/ entretien-dembauche/detail/article/comment-avoir-de-la- repartie-en-entretien-d-embauche.html>
- Denis, S. (2009) *Avoir de la répartie en toutes circonstances.* Paris: Eyrolles.
- Dimier, J. 5 astuces pour avoir de la repartee avec succès ! *Succesrama.com.* [Online]. [Accessed 8 August 2015]. Available from: <http://www.succesrama.com/5-astuces-pour-avoir-de-la- repartie-avec-succes/>
- Le Quintrec, F. (2008) Améliorer sa répartie. *Journaldunet.com.* [Online]. [Accessed 8 August 2015]. Available from: <http://www.journaldunet.com/management/efficacite- personnelle/conseil/ameliorer-sa-repartie/ameliorer-sa-repartie. shtml>
- Luc, D. (2001) L'esprit de répartie : en avoir ou pas. *Psychologie.com.* [Online]. [Accessed 8 August 2015]. Available from: <http://www.psychologies.com/Moi/

IMPROVE YOUR GENERAL KNOWLEDGE

IN A BLINK OF AN EYE !

www.50minutes.com

Made in the USA
Monee, IL
07 July 2026